BRITISH TREES

Angela Royston

Heinemann

Schools Library and Information Services

First published in Great Britain by Heinemann Library
Halley Court, Jordan Hill, Oxford OX2 8EJ
a division of Reed Educational and Professional Publishing Ltd.

Heinemann is a registered trademark of Reed Educational & Professional Publishing Limited.

OXFORD MELBOURNE AUCKLAND
JOHANNESBURG BLANTYRE GABORONE
IBADAN PORTSMOUTH NH CHICAGO

Designed by AMR Ltd.
Printed and bound in Hong Kong/China by South China Printing Co. Ltd.

03 02 01 00
10 9 8 7 6 5 4 3 2 1

ISBN 0 431 00210 X

This title is also available in a hardback library edition (ISBN 0 431 00203 7)

British Library Cataloguing in Publication Data

Royston, Angela
British trees. – (Plants)
1. Trees – Great Britain – Juvenile literature
I. Title
582.1′6′0941

ISBN 0 431 00210 X

Acknowledgements
The Publishers would like to thank the following for permission to reproduce photographs:
Ardea: pp4, 15, 20, B Gibbons p25, C Knights p5, P Morris p16; Bruce Coleman Limited: H Reinhard p8; Garden and Wildlife Matters: pp6, 9, 10, 12, 13, 14, 17, 18, 19, 21, 22, 23, 24, 27, M Collins p26, K Gibson p7; Chris Honeywell: pp28, 29; Tony Stone Images: M Mouchy p11.

Cover photograph: Garden and Wildlife Matters

The publishers would like to thank Dr John Feltwell of Garden Matters for his comments in the preparation of this book.

Every effort has been made to contact copyright holders of any material reproduced in this book. Any omissions will be rectified in subsequent printings if notice is given to the Publisher.

Any words appearing in bold, **like this**, are explained in the Glossary.

Contents

Where trees grow

Trees need plenty of water and fairly good soil to grow. In Britain trees grow in most places except at the top of high mountains or on moors.

Different kinds of trees grow in
different kinds of places, but some
trees, like this hawthorn, grow almost
everywhere.

The mighty oak

Oak trees are one of our most common trees. Long ago, forests of tall oak trees covered much of Britain. Most were cut down to make space to grow **crops**.

Many birds, insects and other animals live in oak trees. These 'oak apples' look like **fruit**, but inside each one a young gall wasp is living and growing.

Common trees

Many common trees grow where their
seeds fall on the ground and take
root. A sycamore tree has winged seeds
which blow a long way in the wind.

In spring this horse chestnut has tall white **flowers** which turn into **conkers** in the autumn. Watch out for their prickly cases!

Street trees

Trees are planted along roads and streets to make the street look nicer. Sometimes the branches are cut to stop the trees growing too tall.

Trees help to clean the air. They take in **carbon dioxide** from traffic fumes and turn it into **oxygen**, which plants and animals breathe.

Garden trees

People plant trees in parks and gardens because they look beautiful. In spring this Japanese cherry tree is covered with pink **flowers**.

People have brought **seeds** to Britain from other parts of the world. Trees like this laburnum tree grow wild in southern Europe.

Fruit trees

Some people plant **fruit** trees in their garden to grow apples, pears or plums. These ripe, juicy pears look ready to eat.

Fruit farmers grow large orchards of apple trees, plum trees or other fruit trees. They sell the fruit to shops and **food-processing** companies.

Exotic trees

Exotic trees grow only in some parts of Britain. Palm trees usually grow in **tropical countries**, but these palms are growing in western Scotland.

Chinese maidenhair trees have leaves shaped like fans. Scientists have found that trees like this grew 200 million years ago, when the dinosaurs lived.

Conifer trees

Conifer trees, such as this pine tree, grow well everywhere. Conifer trees have thin, sharp leaves and produce **cones** instead of **flowers**.

Many conifers grow quickly. They are grown in plantations and then cut down after a few years. Their wood is used to make paper or furniture.

Mountain trees

Mountains are cold, windy places, especially in winter. **Conifer trees** grow well here and so do these small silver birches.

Mountain trees, like this mountain ash, do not need much water and so they are often planted in streets and gardens.

Growing near water

Some kinds of tree grow next to rivers and streams. White willow trees have soft, springy wood which is used to make cricket bats.

The **seeds** of this alder tree will drop into the river and float away. Some of them will drift onto the bank and grow there, lower down the river.

Providing shelter

Trees provide shelter for **crops** and farm animals. This row of poplar trees has been planted around the edge of a dragon-fly **sanctuary**.

Some farmers grow hedges around their fields. Hedges provide homes for wild **flowers** and for birds, mice and insects.

Woodland trees

Some woods have a mixture of
different trees, while others have
mainly one kind of tree. The trees in
this wood are nearly all beech trees.

Many woods are in danger of being cut down to make way for new roads and homes. We need to protect our trees and woods.

How old is that tree?

You can find out how old a living tree is by putting a measuring tape around the trunk. Count one year for every 2 centimetres.

Every year a tree makes a ring of new wood just under the bark. When a tree is cut down you can see these rings on the stump. Count the rings to find out how old the tree is.

Tree map

an English oak tree

ba[rk]

leave[s]

trunk

roots

Glossary

carbon dioxide	a gas which is made when living things breathe out and when fuel is burnt
cone	part of a conifer tree which makes new seeds
conifer tree	a tree which produces new seeds inside cones
conkers	the shiny brown nuts of a horse chestnut tree. They are protected by prickly cases until they are ripe
crops	plants which are grown by farmers for people to eat or use in other ways
exotic trees	trees which originally come from another country
flower	the part of a plant which makes new seeds
food processing	making basic foods, such as fruit, into more advanced foods, like jam or fruit juice
fruit	the part of a plant that holds the ripening seeds
oxygen	a gas which all living things need to breathe to survive
sanctuary	a place that is safe
seed	a seed contains a tiny plant before it begins to grow and a store of food
tropical countries	parts of the world that are hot and wet all year round

Index